CLAIMING
GOD'S
PROMISES

CLAIMING GOD'S PROMISES

A Guide to Discovering Your Spiritual Gifts

Thomas R. Hawkins

Abingdon Press
Nashville

CLAIMING GOD'S PROMISES:
A GUIDE TO DISCOVERING YOUR SPIRITUAL GIFTS

Copyright © 1992 by Abingdon Press

This book is printed on recycled, acid-free paper.

Library of Congress Cataloging-in-Publication Data

Hawkins, Thomas R.
  Claiming God's Promises: a guide to discovering your spiritual gifts/Thomas R. Hawkins.
    p.   cm.
  ISBN 0-687-08397-4 (pbk.: alk. paper)
  1. Spiritual life. 2. Fruit of the Spirit. I. Title
BV4501.2.H36854 1992
234', 13—dc20   92-13015

MANUFACTURED IN THE UNITED STATES OF AMERICA

To
Jan Douberly Hawkins,
friend, companion, gift of God's grace

Contents

Introduction

Last year we received nine new families into our congregation," said pastor Betty Newcomb to her colleagues at the monthly ministerial meeting. "Four of them are already inactive, and at least one other family has never really found a place here. I wish I knew how we could help new members discover a niche for themselves in our church."

"I know what you mean," continued Bob Newell, pastor of a nearby congregation. "We have the same problem. But I'm less and less sure about what to do with the members I already have. Many of them have been serving on the same committees for years. They feel tired and burnt-out.

"As they resign, the nominating committee is having a difficult time replacing them. When we ask people to volunteer for a committee, they turn us down. No one wants to get involved. I wish I knew how I could keep our present membership active, let alone find ways to involve new members."

Pouring himself another cup of coffee, John Rhodes nodded sympathetically. "Our congregation faces the same problems," he started. "We are looking for ways to mobilize our membership, to help both new and old members find places in which they can be involved in ministry.

"But what makes the problem more acute is our recent growth spurt. We have grown to the point where one pastor simply cannot manage all our events, programs, and ministries, as well as preach, counsel, and visit home-bounds.

"Our pastor-parish relations committee wanted to hire an associate pastor. But when we asked our bishop, we were told there is a shortage of candidates. A new position like ours would not be a top priority while some congregations cannot locate pastors," Rhodes said.

"We are exploring ways we can mobilize our laity to pick up the additional work load," he explained. "If we cannot find an ordained associate, then we will have to distribute among lay volunteers some of the functions the paid staff previously performed."

This conversation illustrates at last three reasons why congregations should be interested in helping members discern their spiritual gifts for ministry.

First, some mainline Protestant denominations are facing a critical shortage of qualified pastors. This crisis hit the Roman Catholic Church over a decade ago; Protestant churches are just now beginning to encounter it. The problem stems from long-term demographic shifts in the American population.

Shortly after World War Two, large numbers of young men entered seminaries and became pastors. These pastors are now approaching retirement, and there are not enough new clergy candidates to replace such large classes of retirees. In some denominations, up to 40 percent of the active clergy will be retiring in the next five years.

This pattern will cause critical shortages of trained pastors, and Protestant congregations may discover themselves doing what Roman Catholic churches have already been forced to do: ask the laity to assume duties and responsibilities previously performed by clergy. More than just consumers of programs and ministries, lay people must begin to see themselves as the source of ministries.

As the laity is mobilized to assume these responsibilities, congregations will need a well-defined process for identifying members' gifts for ministry. Both a theological rationale for spiritual gifts and a practical process for discerning these gifts will become crucial. By focusing on discovering spiritual gifts, a congregation can help lay people identify their gifts for ministry.

Second, members volunteer their time and talent to the church when they feel they are receiving something for their effort. Their sense of meaning and purpose is enhanced and enriched through their congregational involvement. People feel burned out or burdened when they can no longer see a connection between who they are as God's people and what they are doing as God's church. A volunteer's hopes, dreams, and values need to be coordinated with the activities in which he or she is asked to participate.

This requires more of a nominating committee than just "filling the slots." Nominating committees have seldom had the volunteer's growth and development as their primary focus. Instead, they have seen their purpose as recruiting people for predefined, institutional roles. The emphasis has been on the institution and its goals rather than on individuals and their purposes.

One long-term result is a declining number of people willing to volunteer. They have felt used or abused by past experiences and are now wary of involvement unrelated to their own personal goals and values. Members lose interest and drop out when they no longer can make a significant connection between who they are and what they are doing.

When congregations help members identify their spiritual gifts for ministry, they are exercising an important form of pastoral care. Volunteering in the church should provide an opportunity for lifelong learning and growth. It should be a means of self-renewal for both congregation and members.

Congregations are responsible for helping members identify their spiritual gifts—the talents, abilities, hopes, and meanings that matter to them. Once members appreciate their unique gifts for ministry, they can better coordinate those gifts with specific church tasks.

Third, many congregations lack an intentional process for involving new members. Some congregations wait passively until the new member initiates his or her own involvement. This system favors the aggressive, extroverted individual, often leaving introverted members feeling they are on the outside looking in.

Other congregations assume that all new members have the same needs and interests. Yet not all newcomers are alike. Not all are interested in the same kinds of involvements and ministries. Nominating committees and pastors routinely put a new member on the first available work group, board, council, or committee just so he or she will "get to know some people."

They never pause to explore any gifts or unique skills the new member possesses. They do not reflect upon how newcomer and congregation might mutually benefit from the new member's gifts and graces. When mismatched with responsibilities, new members may feel they are failures, frustrated by trying to accomplish tasks for which they lack the necessary gifts and graces. Rather than incorporating new members, these processes may in fact hasten them toward inactivity.

Guiding new members through a process of gifts identification can become a powerful means of incorporation into the church. Once new members know their gifts for ministry, they have a better idea about what involvements are appropriate for them. Having new members participate in a gifts workshop or retreat has an added benefit. It enables them to establish bonds with other new members before they move out into the wider congregation.

Guiding new members through a gifts-identification process also communicates that the congregation cares about them as individuals. The congregation is not merely interested in tapping their energy for its ongoing institutional goals. It is concerned for each member's personal growth and development.

How to Use This Book

This resource is designed so that an individual may work through the various sections alone. It is important to stop and complete the exercises that are scattered through the chapters. The exercises help readers make the general concepts and ideas more personal and concrete. Those who take time for the exercises will profit far more than those who simply skip the exercises and continue reading. The object of this resource is not that it be finished as quickly as possible. Rather, the more time and thought invested in reading and reflecting, the greater the dividend.

The book also may be used by a group, with participants doing the reading and exercises between meetings. When the group gathers, a leader may guide the participants through a general discussion of content during the first half of the group session. The second half of the session would allow time for subgroups to discuss the exercise.

Or participants could be asked to do the reading between meetings. The exercises would be completed and discussed by small subgroups at the weekly gathering. At the session's closing, each subgroup could report a summary of its discussion and discovery.

When used in a study or growth group, the following pattern could be adopted:

Week One	Introduction and Chapter 1
Week Two	Chapter 2
Week Three	Chapter 3, first half
Week Four	Chapter 3, second half
Week Five	Chapter 4

Used at a weekend retreat, the resource could be divided into the following sections:

Friday Evening	Introduction and Chapter 1
Saturday Morning	Chapter 2
Saturday Afternoon	Chapter 3, first half
Saturday Evening	Chapter 3, second half
Sunday Morning	Chapter 4

Study guides for each chapter are found in the appendix.

Chapter One

Why Should We Care About Our Spiritual Gifts?

A cross the centuries, the church has taught people to read and learn the Scriptures. It has provided guidelines for moral decision making and for maintaining loving relationships. It has urged us to pray and to seek a contemplative life-style. It has inspired us to serve the needs of the present age, seeking justice and peace.

Yet the church has often failed to help us discern the purposes for which God uniquely creates each of us. It has not always reminded us that discovering our spiritual gifts is fundamental to making a concrete commitment of our lives to Jesus Christ as Lord and Savior. We have not always perceived the connection between exercising our gifts and experiencing communion with God and others. Our spiritual gifts should matter to us for at least four important reasons.

Discovery of our spiritual gifts
helps us to discover our identity.

Men and women are alienated from their own deepest identities when they are unaware of the gifts that make them most uniquely the persons they are. Each of us is a special configuration of experiences, memories, mental abilities, physical attributes, and genetic inheritance. This precise mixture of abilities and experiences has never been before and will never be again in any other man or woman.

When we speak of being true to our spiritual gifts, we are actually talking about being true to our deepest identities.

We cannot be true to ourselves unless we are also true to our gifts. When we cease to be in touch with our God-given gifts and talents, we have lost touch with who we are at our most fundamental level. We have failed to claim that which makes us most uniquely ourselves.

God's love becomes concrete and specific through the unique combination of gifts and talents that God has implanted within each of us. God does not love us in some general or universal way. God loves us concretely by creating within each of us a special configuration of gifts that will never be repeated in anyone else.

When we know and use our gifts, we are doing what only we were created to do. We are being what we alone were created to be. A knowledge of our spiritual gifts undercuts any negative self-image we may have acquired. It reminds us that God loves us through our specific combination of traits, talents, and experiences. If God has created each of us with a unique configuration of gifts and abilities, then we are already precious in God's sight.

"O LORD, thou hast searched me and known me!" sings the psalmist; "Even before a word is on my tongue, lo, O LORD, thou knowest it altogether" (Ps. 139:1, 4). The psalmist confesses an assurance of being shaped by God. Even before birth, unique talents and traits have been implanted into the psalmist's life. God's love is made specific through the bestowal of unique gifts and abilities.

> For thou didst form my inward parts,
> > thou didst knit me together in my mother's womb. . . .
> > My frame was not hidden from thee
> when I was being made in secret,
> > intricately wrought in the depths of the earth.
> Thy eyes beheld my unformed substance;
> > in thy book were written, every one of them,
> the days that were formed for me.   (Ps. 139:13, 15-16)

Similarly, the prophets sensed that God had shaped their vocation before their birth. God had woven their prophetic identity into the very fabric of their existence. God's Word came to Jeremiah: "Before I formed you in the womb I knew you, and before you were born I consecrated you; I appointed you a prophet to the nations" (Jer. 1:5). As much as Jeremiah might have wanted to escape from his identity and gifts, he could not do so while still remaining true to himself.

The Bible repeats the same story again and again. Jonah tried to flee from his prophetic call and identity. He ended up in the depths of the sea, where he repented and accepted his task and call. Isaiah, Moses, Miriam, Lydia, and others disclosed the same pattern in their lives and ministries.

This suggests that identity, spiritual gifts, and our daily work are intimately related. Our work is an outward and visible expression of our inward spiritual gifts. What we do flows from who we are. What we make with our hands, what we do with our time, and what we construct with our imagination and creativity are outward manifestations of our inward spiritual lives.

Our work is an expression of our deepest identity. Joseph Conrad understood this connection when he wrote in *The Heart of Darkness*, "I like what is in the work—the chance to find yourself. Your own reality—for yourself and not for others—what no other man can ever know."

Many men and women have lost touch with this connection between work and identity. They work only to earn a living. They do not have a vocation or a profession; they have only an occupation—tasks that occupy their time until they can do as they please with whatever time and energy remain. No longer is their skill or ability seen as a divine gift bestowed upon them to which their daily work bears witness in the world.

When we no longer see our work as an expression of our unique identity or as an exercise of our special gifts, we begin to define our selfhood in other ways. We are what we possess. Our possessions define who we are. The more we have, the more we can consume, the greater our sense of selfhood.

Another consequence is the mad steeplechase to find an ultimate meaning in activities beyond work. We plan frantic vacations during which we overschedule our time, attempting to find some momentary enjoyment in an otherwise drab, empty life. We distract ourselves with amusements and entertainments, hoping to find the stimulation we cannot discover during our working hours. If we cannot find joy and meaning in our work, then at least we can use the money we earn to buy ourselves some pleasure.

These paths to selfhood, however, lead us nowhere. The only ultimate path to our identity is through the discovery of those special gifts which our Creator has embedded within our unique social experiences and genetic inheritance.

We need to discover our spiritual gifts because they define our essential identity. When we exercise our gifts, we are giving meaning to our daily work, relationships, and leisure. The discerning of our gifts, however, leads us to another discovery. It provides us with a pathway to communion between God and our true selves.

EXERCISE ONE

Our family inheritance is part of that unique configuration of experiences and abilities through which God claims us. The following exercise is meant to help you begin to identify your gifts by reflecting on your family and life experiences.

Draw a time line of your life in the space. At one end, mark the year you were born. Then divide the line into five-year segments, continuing the line until you will be eighty years old.

With colored markers or crayons, locate all the important events of your life to this point: major events, hospitalizations, illnesses, birth of children or siblings, conversion, baptism, school events, marriage, career events, death of parents or friends . . .

Now take some time to reflect on what this map says about your unique experiences and perspectives. What colors did you use? Blues are sometimes seen as cool colors and may indicate a detached attitude about life. Oranges, yellows, and reds are hot or warm colors which sometimes denote a passion for life. What colors did you pick for which events? What does this say?

What patterns do you see? Cycles and rhythms? Turning points? Stepping-stone events that build to the next?

One of the most important steps in identifying your gifts is to have some clear sense of God's call—the purpose or vision for which God has claimed you. Does the time line suggest any overarching theme, vision, or purpose in your life?

Discovery of our gifts helps us to know
God's will for our lives.

God's will for our lives is not written in some inscrutable handwriting that eludes our grasp; it is written into the very fabric of our being. It is found in the particular combination of experiences, talents, abilities, genetic inheritance, wounds, and failures that make us who we are.

What does God want me to do with my life? How can I hear God's call? Can I ever know God's plan for my life, or even God's intentions in this current situation? The answer does not lie in seeking some obscure sign. We will not discover God's will by creating special tests or looking for hidden meanings and messages.

Sometimes we look for God's will in the wrong places and in the wrong ways. Some Christians speak of "putting out a fleece" as a way to discern God's will in a particular situation. Just as Gideon used a fleece to test God's purposes, they set up some conditions that will reveal God's plan (see Judg. 6:36-40). If I see two brown dogs on my walk this morning, though I usually see none, then God must want me to purchase that new car. When all is said and done, such methods seldom satisfy our yearning to know what God desires.

Sometimes we seek God's will in the Scriptures. We close our eyes, let the Bible fall open, and place our finger on the page. The verse upon which our finger rests reveals God's will for our lives. Yet it remains unclear whether we are reading our will into the text or actually discovering God's will from it.

We often struggle to know God's will, but we seldom look in the most obvious place. We make discerning God's will much more difficult than it really is.

> It is not in heaven, that you should say,
> "Who will go up for us to heaven, and
> bring it to us, that we may hear it and
> do it?" Neither is it beyond the sea,
> that you should say, "Who will go over the
> sea for us, and bring it to us, that we may
> hear it and do it?" But the word is very
> near you; it is in your mouth and in
> your heart, so that you can do it.
>   (Deut. 30:12-14)

God's will is not in heaven or beyond the sea but as near as our mouths and our hearts. It is embedded in the unique configuration of gifts with which we were created.

It is revealed to us in our gifts and talents: "We ask to know the will of God without guessing that [God's] will is written into our very beings. We perceive that will when we discern our gifts. Our obedience and surrender to God are in large part our obedience and surrender to our gifts" (O'Connor, p. 15).

The God who created us implanted a unique configuration of gifts within us. When we identify and acknowledge our gifts, we discover the Creator God who made us for divine-human communion. To know our spiritual gifts is to know the God who created us for divine communion through our specific abilities and talents.

Writing to one of his spiritual directees, Abbe de Tourville said that God creates and molds a specific world of abilities which constitutes our self. This configuration does not merely reveal our deepest identity; it also mirrors the God who created us: "You carry a whole world within your soul always. . . . It is the world of God . . . for whom for various reasons and in varying degrees, you are the true child through the special nature of the grace which has been given to you" (de Tourville, p. 24). To discern our gifts is to discover God's unique will for our lives. To uncover our spiritual gifts opens us to new levels of personal communion with our Creator.

EXERCISE TWO ≡≡≡≡≡≡

This exercise also focuses upon family. What values have you received from your family experiences that continue to shape and gift you? Which are values that once may have been appropriate but no longer really serve you well? Use the space below to record your thoughts.

Complete the following chart. Family sayings are those messages, sayings, family stories, or myths that you heard again and again. Write them down in the column labeled "Family Sayings." Then ask yourself what "ought" or "ought-not" messages were embedded in those sayings. Finally, what are the more basic values they reflect?

For example, I grew up in a family where we heard a common saying: "Hard work never hurt anyone." The "ought" message was that I should work hard and not complain. The "ought-not" message was that you are lazy if you don't work hard. Its positive value was a commitment to quality and competence; its negative value was that it encouraged one to be a workaholic.

Once you have completed the chart, spend some time thinking about how the messages and their values may have affected your unique configuration of talents, abilities, and purposes.

Family Sayings	Family "Oughts"	Family "Ought-Nots"	Positive Values	Negative Values

Discovery of our gifts guides the ways we can commit our lives to God.

As long as we do not know our special talents and gifts, we can keep our religious commitments vague and general, and thus our lives and our values are not genuinely challenged by God's call. We can remain only hearers of the Word, not doers. We can enjoy religious emotions and have spiritual highs without committing ourselves concretely to God.

As long as we do not name our unique, God-given talents, we can avoid committing those gifts—and our time, energy, and resources along with them—to God's purposes in the world. We can have religious experiences without responding to God's specific claim upon our lives.

"Commitment at the point of my gifts means that I must give up being a straddler. Somewhere in the depths of me I know this. Life will not be the smorgasbord I have made it, sampling and tasting here and there. My commitment will give me an identity," says Elizabeth O'Connor. "But I do not like the sound of this. I do not want to be boxed in" (O'Connor, p. 43).

When we have identified our gifts, all this changes. If I know that God has implanted a special gift for teaching within me, then I cannot ignore the call to teach the junior-high Sunday school class. This concrete commitment of time and energy may even mean that my whole week's schedule must be rearranged.

If I recognize that I have an ability to understand and comfort those who are grieving, then I cannot continue to see my religious journey as a private affair that excludes others. Claiming my gift may radically transform my life. It may open my daily routine to constant rearrangement.

If I realize I have the gift of administration—knowing how to organize projects and see them to completion with a minimum of conflict and confusion—then I must commit myself to using this talent. Acknowledging and claiming this God-given talent, however, may mean that I no longer can be a passive consumer of someone else's programs.

When we name our gift, we cannot remain as uncommitted as we once were. Yet God ultimately did not make our souls to be passive and without purpose. We were made for action. We were made to commit our lives to our Creator and Redeemer. Through such commitments, we are restored to the joy of divine communion.

Committing ourselves to the use of our God-given gifts will ultimately open us to receive the joy and communion for which our souls were created. "The soul is made for action, and cannot rest till it be employed," wrote Thomas Traherne. "If therefore you would be happy, your life must be as full of operation as God of treasure" (Traherne, Book IV, 95).

EXERCISE THREE ═══════════

Close your eyes and think back to your childhood and youth. Who were your heroes and heroines? What men and women did you admire and look up to? Did you want to grow up to be just like someone?

In the columns to the right, list the qualities or abilities that you admired in those men and women.

For example, I admired my grandfather. He was a social worker and public-assistance administrator. As a child, I would ride in his car as he visited the people who received assistance for the blind, old-age pensions, or public aid. He was always considerate and cared deeply about people. The values I saw in him were compassion and commitment to society's weakest members. The abilities he possessed were a willingness to listen carefully to others and the skill to be a good negotiator and administrator.

As I reflect upon my childhood heroes and heroines, I realize that I admired in them the qualities that I hoped I also would some day possess. I wanted to emulate those people because I instinctively knew that they and I had something in common (this exercise inspired by Edwards, pp. 55-58).

After you list your heroes and heroines, reflect on how this might also be true of your life.

Discovery of our gifts guides us toward sanctification.

God's *prevenient* grace implants certain spiritual gifts into the very fabric of our existence. God's *justifying* grace is active as we acknowledge those gifts, committing our lives to God in all our specificity and uniqueness. By the same token, God's *sanctifying* grace operates in our lives through our spiritual gifts.

Through sanctification, the Holy Spirit continues to root out sin from our lives. Sanctifying grace empowers us to grow in centeredness and wholeness. Exercising our spiritual gifts assists the Spirit's sanctification of our lives. As we claim our gifts, we must confront and overcome our lives' sinful dynamics.

From Dante's *Inferno* to Chaucer's *Canterbury Tales*, envy always has been one of the seven deadly sins. When we are envious of others, we generally do not appreciate our own uniqueness and self-worth. We are envious of people who have developed their gifts, while we cannot even name our own. Conversely, we do not have time to discern our own gifts when our energy is dissipated by yearning for someone else's.

Envy manifests itself in at least two ways. *Immobilizing* envy occurs when we do not try to cut the other person down to our size but instead feel helpless and impotent. We internalize the envy. We feel we have no worth and cannot make a difference in the world. We do not bother to initiate action because we feel inferior and worthless.

Aggressive envy, on the other hand, seeks revenge on those who possess the qualities we want but seem to lack. It can lead to the sins of violence and anger. Cain's envy sought bloody revenge against Abel: Whereas Abel had discovered his unique God-given gift and was rewarded for exercising it, Cain could not identify what he should offer as his most precious sacrifice to God. Cain's envy led him to murder his brother. He unleashed the dynamic of envy that repeats itself throughout Scripture in the story of Joseph and his brothers, of David and King Saul, or of Simon Magus and the apostles.

Using our God-given talents, on the other hand, helps us come to terms with envy's destructiveness. When we envy others, it is almost always because we are not valuing ourselves and what we are doing. Identifying our spiritual gifts unleashes the sanctifying grace that helps root out envy from our lives. We no longer need to envy others when we are truly exercising our own unique gifts.

Greed also has been considered one of the seven deadly sins. Greed seeks to possess something far beyond what is needed. It is not so much the love of possessions as the love of possessing. As Capps says, "Greed is ambition and purpose that have no limits, that follow no commonly agreed upon rules and guidelines" (Capps, p. 37).

Knowing our gifts frees us from the greedy need to possess every possible gift. Not knowing which gifts are truly our own, we want them all. Not knowing which purposes are uniquely ours, we desire to achieve them all. Yet no matter how many gifts we greedily attempt to possess, only those truly our own can grant us joy and communion with God. Greed loses its grip over us when we discover our special gifts and the life mission for which God has intended us.

When David first prepared to battle Goliath, King Saul suggested that he put on the king's own armor, which would protect David against Goliath's blows. David took Saul's advice and put it on, but it was too big and heavy for him. It did not fit his body. It was not appropriate for the battle he planned to pursue. David felt awkward, incapable of moving freely.

So he ordered the king's armor-bearers to remove it. He then went to the stream bed, selected five smooth stones, and took out the sling he had learned to use as a shepherd.

Employing his unique gifts, David defeated Goliath. Saul's armor, as useful as it was to Saul, was a hindrance to David (see I Sam. 17:38-40).

We sometimes fail to perceive what David instinctively knew. We long for someone else's armor and achievements. We greedily seek that person's talents, believing we can defeat our giants if we are using their gifts. Yet it never works. We cannot put on someone else's gifts. We can effectively utilize only our own.

Greed for another's armor, achievements, or gifts becomes a terrible burden. Instead of protecting us, it imprisons and entraps us. When we name and exercise our own gifts, we can let go of our greedy yearning for someone else's talents and achievements.

When we properly value our own gifts, it also helps us avoid becoming proud and arrogant. Pride is not to be confused with legitimate self-esteem. In fact, self-esteem and pride are opposites. Those who are proud often lack self-esteem. Unsure of our genuine worth, we claim to be more than we feel we already are. Sometimes we even accept this false image as our real self. We believe we are self-made men and women—we have done it all on our own.

Focusing on our God-given gifts, however, helps God's grace to break through this wall of pride. Our gifts are not really our own but come as an unexpected gift from beyond ourselves. This realization demolishes our prideful, self-sufficient image. Our lives are not really our own. What is mine, cries Paul, that I have not received? (I Cor. 4:7b).

Our spiritual gifts remind us that we are not self-made. When we are using our gifts, we are really giving to God the only thing we have to give. We did not produce our talents and abilities. We did not create the natural resources with which we work. We create out of the gifts with which God has blessed us. There is little room for pride when this realization begins to shape our lives.

Moreover, pride isolates us from others. We believe we are self-sufficient, and our self-centeredness blinds us to our bonds with others and with our Creator. We often describe proud people as aloof and inaccessible. The proud deny both their need for others and their obligations to others.

Yet God embeds our gifts within us so that we may be God's co-creators in the upbuilding of community and creation. Our gifts are not given to us for our private pleasure and amusement. They are given for service and sharing. Pride fosters isolation; but an awareness of our gifts nourishes commitments that relate us to others. When we claim and develop our spiritual gifts, we release the Spirit's sanctifying grace which calls us beyond self-centeredness to a God-centered life.

Conclusion

One important way the Holy Spirit is active in our lives is through discovering and employing our gifts. Through God's prevenient grace, God implants certain talents and abilities in us which give us our unique identity and vocation in life. The Spirit's justifying grace moves us to the point of acknowledging God's will for our lives and committing our lives to God through the acknowledgment of our gifts. Throughout our continuing Christian growth, the Spirit's sanctifying grace guides us to wholeness and centeredness. As we exercise our gifts, we confront the sinful dynamics that lock us into patterns of anger, greed, envy, pride, and sloth.

Chapter Two

What Does the Bible Say About Gifts?

G ifts played an important role in the early Christian communities. They were especially important in the Pauline churches. Unfortunately, these churches took the role of gifts so much for granted that Paul never bothered to explain or discuss them in his letters and writings. Things that everyone knows and accepts are seldom mentioned in correspondence and conversation. The New Testament assumes a great deal about gifts but says very little directly about them. Nonetheless, we can glean some information from the two or three passages in Paul's letters which explicitly mention gifts.

The basis for all gifts is the gift of grace through Christ.

Paul's belief that God gives spiritual gifts for ministry developed from one fundamental conviction: God's ultimate spiritual gift has already been given in Jesus' death and resurrection. Acceptance of this saving gift opens up the possibility of life in the Spirit. Our subsequent participation in Christ through the Holy Spirit empowers us to receive spiritual gifts for ministry.

Spiritual gifts are "grace gifts." Grace and gifts are intertwined throughout the New Testament. The Greek words for *grace (charis)* and *gift (charism)* share the same root. To receive the gift of God's salvation in Jesus Christ is to receive God's grace. Paul makes this connection in Romans 5:15-17:

But the free gift is not like the trespass. For if many died through one man's trespass, much more have the grace of God and the free gift in the grace of that one man Jesus Christ abounded for many. And the free gift is not like the effect of that one man's sin. For the judgment following one trespass brought condemnation, but the free gift following many trespasses brings justification. If, because of one man's trespass, death reigned through that one man, much more will those who receive the abundance of grace and the free gift of righteousness reign in life through the one man Jesus Christ.

The words *gift* and *grace* occur eight times in this brief passage. They define and reinforce each other, being so tightly bound that Paul cannot think about one apart from the other.

For Paul, all discussion of gifts must start with God's gracious gift of salvation through Jesus Christ. The Holy Spirit is the concrete pledge of God's gift of salvation. Our life in Christ results in other spiritual gifts for ministry, but we cannot receive these practical gifts for ministry unless our response of praise and thanksgiving first acknowledges God's gracious gift of salvation.

In Romans 6:23, Paul contrasts the "wages" of sin with the "free gift" of salvation through Christ: "For the wages of sin is death, but the free gift of God is eternal life in Christ Jesus our Lord." When we merited condemnation and punishment, says Paul, God gave the free gift of eternal life. Grace is God's gift to us.

We, in turn, return a gift to God: our hearts, our praise, and our thanksgiving. God offers the gift of grace; we offer the gift of our hearts. The circle of giving is then completed. This mutual gift-giving establishes a communion, a new loving relationship, between ourselves and God. It is a relationship in Christ through the Holy Spirit.

Paul's spiritual gifts, or gifts for ministry, flow from this gracious communion of love. Specific gifts are intended to nurture our continued life in the Spirit. They enable us to share in God's ongoing redemption of the world.

We cannot, however, receive these spiritual gifts for ministry unless we first accept the gift of new life in Christ Jesus. "Gratefulness makes us graceful in a double sense. In gratefulness we open ourselves to this gratuitous universe and so we become fully graced with it. And in doing so we learn to move gracefully with its flow as in a universal dance" (Steindl-Rast 1984, p. 201).

We often seek God's lesser gifts as ends in themselves. We should instead be seeking the Giver, not the gifts. Attempts to identify our spiritual gifts and exercise them for ministry will end in failure unless we remember this important starting point.

We will discover our spiritual gifts for ministry along the way, as a by-product of seeking personal communion with God. Our spiritual gifts are always a consequence of our acceptance of God's greatest gift, the saving death and resurrection of Jesus Christ.

Paul explicitly discusses spiritual gifts, or gifts for ministry, in two passages. But Romans 12 and First Corinthians 12 can be understood only in light of this prior relationship between salvation, grace, and gifts.

Our spiritual gifts result from our salvation by faith through grace. Through faith in Christ, we receive the gift of the Holy Spirit in the church: "Since we are justified by faith, we have peace with God through our Lord Jesus Christ. Through him we have obtained access to this grace in which we stand. . . . God's love has been poured into our hearts through the Holy Spirit which has been given to us" (Rom. 5:1-2, 5).

There are different gifts, but one Spirit.
(First Corinthians 12)

Paul's earliest written discussion of spiritual gifts appears in First Corinthians 12. Paul's relationship to the Corinthian church was a stormy one. After Paul's departure, the Corinthians had embraced other conflicting interpretations of the gospel and spiritual gifts. The letters reflect his attempt to correct their belief that spiritual gifts were personal possessions that bestowed individual status and detached Christians from their responsibility for this world.

The Corinthians had turned away from the radical mutuality of the gospel, replacing it with an emphasis upon status, privilege, and prestige. The celebration of the Lord's Supper was no longer a place of mutuality and reciprocity. It had become a place where distinctions between rich and poor, privileged and not-so-privileged were affirmed rather than overcome. The well-to-do came early and consumed all the good food and wine before the lower-class members could arrive (see I Cor. 11:17-22.)

This status-seeking had extended beyond the congregation's sacramental life into its ministry and mission. Members were making distinctions between certain offices and functions, regarding some as conferring more prestige than others. Hierarchy and privilege were replacing partnership and equality. Some gifts for ministry had attained greater status than others, and those who possessed these gifts lorded it over the others.

The emphasis upon individual status had obscured the communal nature of Christian faith. The Corinthians regarded the individual believer as the only place Christ's Spirit could dwell. Seeing their individual bodies as the Spirit's dwelling place, they had forgotten that the Spirit's true temple was the whole community of faith. They had ceased to see themselves as members of the one Body of Christ.

The Corinthians believed that God had given them spiritual gifts for their own self-gratification rather than for the building up of their common life as Christ's Body, the church. Having lost sight of their common participation in the one Body of Christ, they interpreted spiritual gifts as special qualities given for personal enjoyment. Gifts were reduced to signs of personal status and prestige.

The Corinthians also had adopted a dualistic interpretation of Christian faith. Spirit and matter were set in opposition. The Spirit had nothing to do with material life. When they experienced the Spirit, they were being lifted out of this corrupt, material world. The mundane, everyday world was devalued and discounted. Paul's discussion of spiritual gifts addressed all these issues.

First, he reminded the Corinthians that while a variety of gifts exist, all are of equal value. Because they all come from God, they are all of equal importance; no gift confers more status or more privilege than another. "There are varieties of gifts, but the same Spirit; and there are varieties of service, but the same Lord; and there are varieties of working, but it is the same God who inspires them all in every one" (I Cor. 12:4-6).

There is no room for pride. Christians should not compare their gifts. The Spirit has apportioned all gifts according to the mystery of God's call and claim upon our lives. Rather than feeling proud, we have every reason to accept our gift with humility. Whatever gift we have received, we have done nothing to deserve it.

We played no part in determining our gifts for ministry, and therefore we should not overvalue them or compare them to those of someone else. "All these are activated by one and the same Spirit, who allots to each one individually" (I Cor. 12:11 NRSV).

Paul's extended metaphor of the body and its members drives home this same point. No single limb or organ can claim superiority over another bodily part. In fact, those parts that seem weaker or less honorable receive greater attention than the others.

This passage reinforces the early church's radical mutuality and partnership: "God has so composed the body, giving the greater honor to the inferior part, that there may be no discord in the body, but that the members may have the same care for one another. If one member suffers, all suffer together; if one member is honored, all rejoice together" (I Cor. 12:24b-26).

Second, Paul reminded the Corinthians that gifts are given for ministries to the community. God calls us to vocations of service and gives us the gifts needed to fulfill those ministries. In fact, Paul used different words—*charism, vocation,* and *service*—that point to the same reality.

First Corinthians 12:4-6 alternates *charism* with *service;* the two words are treated as equivalent terms. Similarly, Romans 11 and First Corinthians 7:7 use *charism* and *vocation* interchangeably. "In its widest sense, [charism] signifies *the call of God, addressed to an individual, to a particular ministry in the community, which brings with it the ability to fulfil that ministry*" (Küng, p. 247). The key question thus becomes: Does someone else experience the grace of God when I employ my gift for ministry? Is my spiritual gift a means of grace in someone else's life?

Third, Paul stressed that the spiritual and the material are not separate realities. Instead, manifestations of Spirit are to be found in conduct and service. The Spirit materializes in concrete, practical gifts for ministry. Spiritual gifts do not take Christians out of this world; they provide a way we can live the life of Christ in the midst of a material world. God's Spirit becomes incarnate in services and ministries that employ our charisms for the renewal of God's creation.

We are manifesting the Spirit's power in our lives when we exercise our special gifts for ministry. God's reign is not just a heavenly realm beyond this material world. We are making God's reign visible whenever we respond to God's call, employing our gifts for ministry. Our gifts are given so that we may share in God's ongoing healing of a broken creation. Far from lifting us out of this world, our spiritual gifts drive us into the heart of our world and its needs. As Küng states:

> Charisms are the revelations, in concrete and individual form, of the *charis*, the power of God's grace, which takes hold of us, leads us to our appointed service and gives us an individual share in the reign of Christ. And to the extent that we have a present share in the grace and the reign of Christ in the Spirit, our charisms are expressions of power . . . "the manifestation of the Spirit" (I Cor. 12:6f.).
>
> (Küng, p. 248, italics mine)

Finally, Paul provided a brief list of spiritual gifts. One cannot regard this as a complete or exhaustive list. In fact, Paul's lists in Romans and First Corinthians vary in the specific gifts mentioned and in the ranking of those that do repeat themselves. He simply named those gifts for ministry that came immediately to his mind as he illustrated his point.

What remains important, however, is the diversity of gifts he listed. Gifts for ministry are diverse because the church's needs are always diverse. As the church adapts to new cultures and environments, it will always need new gifts to fulfill its ministries of reconciliation and healing.

EXERCISE ONE

Below is a list of twenty-one gifts mentioned in Romans, First Corinthians, Ephesians, and elsewhere. Please note that these are not listed in any particular priority or importance. If you see one of these that describes you, take a few moments to write how and when you used this gift. Then ask yourself how frequently you exercise this gift.

GIFT	TIME I USED THIS GIFT RECENTLY	HOW OFTEN I USE IT
1. Administration (plan, achieve goals)		
2. Mercy (have compassion for the suffering or aged and meet their needs)		
3. Teaching (communicate God's Word to others)		
4. Healing (ability to heal others)		
5. Knowledge (ability to study, analyze, retain information, and communicate it)		
6. Tongues (speak in unknown languages)		

GIFT	TIME I USED THIS GIFT RECENTLY	HOW OFTEN I USE IT
7. Miracles (perform super- human acts that embody the gospel)		
8. Helping (sense someone's need and offer support)		
9. Celibacy (remain single so as to have total energy for serving God)		
10. Missionary (adapt to new culture and translate gospel into its terms)		
11. Exhortation (support, strengthen those whose faith is weak or tested)		
12. Serving (perform tasks that meet others' needs)		

GIFT	TIME I USED THIS GIFT RECENTLY	HOW OFTEN I USE IT
13. Hospitality (welcome strangers, make people feel at home)		
14. Faith (witness to God's will despite feelings or circumstances, so as to strengthen others' faith)		
15. Wisdom (insight into God's ways and people's lives to help people)		
16. Interpretation of Tongues (interpret one who speaks in tongues)		
17. Evangelism/Preaching (proclaim good news to move people to commitment)		

GIFT	TIME I USED THIS GIFT RECENTLY	HOW OFTEN I USE IT
18. Giving (share one's resources with joy to spread good news, benefit others)		
19. Prophecy (speak God's will as it judges a situation and calls people to change)		
20. Pastoring (shepherd, counsel, support people in their Christian growth)		
21. Discernment (judge whether a spirit is of God or of the evil one)		

Once you have competed the list, go back and select the five items that most strongly characterize your Christian life. Write them in the space below:

Now write a few sentences describing where you might put these gifts to work in a more intentional, faithful way.

Paul illustrates variations on a theme.
(Romans 12 and Ephesians 4)

Spiritual gifts, or gifts for ministry, are mentioned in two other New Testament letters: Romans and Ephesians. Paul wrote his letter to the Romans for very different purposes than he wrote his Corinthian letters. Romans was a letter of introduction to a congregation he hoped to visit. He therefore presented a summary of his beliefs in order to validate his ministry. The letter to the Ephesians, on the other hand, is devoid of a personal greeting and does not discuss any specific matters of faith and practice. Partly because of this, it may be a general letter to a number of churches, to which Paul or one of his intimate disciples is presenting a summary of faith.

Both letters echo the themes found in First Corinthians 12. Here, however, they are presented in shorter, less polemic passages. Paul urged the Romans not to see their special gifts for ministry as a source of pride: "I say to everyone among you not to think of yourself more highly than you ought" (12:3 NRSV).

At the same time, they were not to think *less* of themselves than they ought. They were not to devalue their gifts but use them for the community's service. A realistic acceptance of one's spiritual gifts is an antidote against both pride and low self-esteem.

Paul employed the image of the body and its members to express the interdependence, equality, and mutuality of Christians and their gifts: "For as in one body we have many members, and all the members do not have the same function, so we, though many, are one body in Christ . . . . Having gifts [*charism*] that differ according to the grace [*charis*] given to us, let us use them" (Rom. 12:4-6).

Paul again stressed that God gives spiritual gifts for the upbuilding of the church, not for individual enjoyment and self-gratification. If one compares Romans 12 to the third major discussion of gifts in Ephesians 4, the emphasis on community service is made even more forcefully:

And [God's] gifts were that some should be apostles, some prophets, some evangelists, some pastors and teachers, to equip the saints for the work of ministry, for building up the body of Christ, until we all attain to the unity of the faith and of the knowledge of the Son of God . . . to the measure of the stature of the fulness of Christ. (Eph. 4:11-13)

God gives individual Christians gifts so that they may equip the whole church for sharing in the one ministry of Christ.

Moreover, the upbuilding of the Christian community is not an end in itself. Rather, the church is a parable of reconciliation and healing in a broken, alienated world. As the church lives out its vocation in the world, ever-widening circles of wholeness will expand to encompass all the universe.

Gifts are for the upbuilding of the Christian community in the short-term. In the long run, they are for the healing of the whole cosmos: "To make everyone see what is the plan of the mystery hidden for ages in God who created all things; so that through the church the wisdom of God in its rich variety might now be made known to the rulers and authorities in the heavenly places" (Eph. 3:9-10 NRSV).

Spiritual gifts are given so that the Spirit may transform our material world through the ministry of God's people. The Holy Spirit concretizes itself in the world when we use our spiritual gifts. Our ministry and service bear witness to the Spirit's power in our world. Spiritual gifts make us more aware of the world's needs and hungers. They do not turn us away from the world and its problems.

The New Testament Church and Today's Church

What do these passages suggest about spiritual gifts and the contemporary church? How can we create congregations that develop, nurture, and manifest spiritual gifts?

First, one of the church's major tasks is to help people discover their gifts. Elizabeth O'Connor states the issue emphatically: "A primary purpose of the Church is to help us discover our gifts and, in the face of our fears, to hold us accountable for them so that we can enter into the joy of creating" (O'Connor, p. 17). The church is healthy when all the people are sharing their gifts to meet others' needs. Christ is at work in our world where such diversity of gifts and oneness of Spirit prevails.

Church nominating committees sometimes ask the wrong questions when they are enlisting volunteers. They usually begin with a chart of offices or tasks that need to be done. They begin with the church's needs and look for people who can fulfill those responsibilities. Seldom do they begin with the church's membership list and ask, "What kind of church experience would help each person grow personally and spiritually?"

Paul's emphasis on spiritual gifts challenges church nominating committees to begin with each individual's gifts rather than with the institution's goals and purposes. Nominating committees can help church members identify their own gifts. They then can find ways those gifts and the church's purposes will mutually complement each other.

This involves much more than frantically filling slots on a church election slate a few weeks before the annual meeting. A church nominating committee is fulfilling its ministry when it finds ways for members to identify and employ their gifts in ways that foster spiritual growth.

Churches are places where people can experience the personal and spiritual growth that result from people being and doing that for which God created them. Some authors, like O'Connor, might go so far as to say that this is the church's sole responsibility: If the church does this task effectively, then all its other functions will automatically work smoothly. Christ's ministry is taking place in the world when all God's people have identified and are using their gifts.

Second, these passages challenge many of our assumptions about leadership and administration. Members possess different gifts, but all are equally important for Christ's witness in the world. There is no room for the proud who lord it over others (Mark 10:42-45). Nor should anyone feel that his or her gifts are less valuable than another's.

Many congregations have an unofficial hierarchy. Those who make policy are at the "top," and those who do the work are on the "bottom." Real power is seen as being lodged in those who serve on administrative committees such as finance, trustees, or the governing board. The "workers" are left to staff the church school, run the annual bazaar, serve on the work-day crew, or cook at church suppers.

Long-term members serve on policy and administrative committees; newer members usually are restricted to the worker roles. Often those who serve on administrative committees feel they have greater wisdom, status, or power than the workers. Such church systems fail to manifest the radical mutuality and fluid roles that Paul's letters envision.

Frequently there is an informal "promotion system." If someone is a worker long enough, he or she may potentially become a leader. Unfortunately, the church always needs more workers than leaders, so only a few workers will be promoted as leaders. The remaining workers often feel they have been exploited. If they are not invited to become leaders, they may become inactive, refusing to implement programs they had no role in determining or governing. They are left feeling their gifts are less important than those of the "leaders."

Congregations foster spiritual gifts for ministry when they see differences as a source of strength rather than as a problem. Too often, we see different gifts and talents as a problem to be solved. We rank our differences, arranging them into categories of better and worse, more important and less significant, stronger and weaker. We want to prioritize our differences so that life feels more predictable and secure. Different abilities are translated into differences in excellence and value.

Our congregations might discover renewed power, however, if they saw different gifts as mutually complementary rather than as something to prioritize. Our differences can help us overcome personal limitations: "In mutuality, we count on our differences to release new resources in our midst. . . . Our differences in strength can bind us in effective social life. It is because we are not all the same that we need one another" (Whitehead and Whitehead, p. 87).

This means we should select leaders and workers on the basis of who can best grow through the use of a gift appropriate to that office. Offices and positions should not automatically go to those who "deserve" them because of status, power, or prestige. This means electing to our governing boards those who can best administer and coordinate the congregation's life rather than those who want to be there because they desire or "deserve" the status or prestige.

Congregations that take spiritual gifts seriously will put the church finances into the hands of those who can best manage financial accounts, not those who want to possess the power of the purse. These same congregations do not ask if someone has "been around long enough" to serve on a board of trustees. Nominating committees take gifts seriously when they ask who has the talent for a task rather than who deserves an assignment because it's "their turn."

Congregations that have rediscovered Paul's radical mutuality no longer regard some committees as more important than others. Being a member of the social-concerns committee or the education commission is not seen as less important or prestigious than being on the governing board or the trustees. The central issue is not status and prestige but where one's unique abilities can best serve the whole church.

When we recognize the variety of spiritual gifts, we will see leadership as something fluid and changing. Someone who is a leader on one project may become a worker in another. The gifts that made someone an appropriate leader for one program may not be suited for leadership in the next project.

Churches that take gifts seriously will be prepared for unexpected role reversals. Leaders will become workers; workers can become leaders. Long-term members will take their cues from newer members, and newcomers will follow the direction of those who have been members all their lives.

Workers are allowed the initiative to make decisions about those programs and policies that directly impact them. Each person in a group may have a specific leadership task and be called upon to exercise it, depending upon the group's needs at any particular moment.

Third, God gives complementary gifts. This means that I will discover my gifts only when you are free to discover yours. I can find my identity only as I help you claim and nurture your own. My growth is linked to your growth even as your development is dependent upon mine. The locus for this mutuality is the church as Christ's living Body, as the Household of the Holy Spirit.

Our words *community* and *communion* derive from the Latin *munio*, meaning to "build" or "fortify." Therefore, a community is a mutual building, a building with (*communio*) others. The church is where we mutually build up one another.

> Through our use of our gifts in service to others, we ourselves reach maturity, and the body of Christ is built up and unified, made whole. . . .
>
> The church [is] a community of persons who are called to grow in unity with one another by serving one another, each one using his or her gift and each one valuing the gifts of others. (Edwards, p. 23)

The exercising of our unique talents is not meant for self-gratification or for demonstrating our competence and accomplishment. The Spirit empowers our gifts so that we may enable one another's growth in Christ. We are undervaluing ourselves and our gifts when we do not use them to enrich the church's ministry and witness.

The regular rotation of offices forces people to grow, to discover talents they may have forgotten they possess. It also allows others new opportunities for discovering their gifts and abilities. I need to let go of some things I am doing so that you may have an opportunity to test *your* talents and discover *your* gifts.

Fourth, Ephesians emphasizes the church's role in healing the whole cosmos. This challenges us to validate those ministries that serve the larger community and world as well as those that maintain the church's internal structures and programs. Gifts are not given to maintain the church as an institution. They are given for the healing of the whole world. The Spirit is not at work just inside the church's walls. God's Spirit hovers over the world's chaos, seeking to restore harmony and wholeness.

The church has sometimes fostered a ghetto mentality. Too often we have seen the church as the only valid arena for exercising ministry. We regard those who invest their energy in community development, political life, or ministry in their workplace as somehow neglecting their responsibility to share their time, talent, gifts, and service with the church. We see other community groups as our competitors rather than as partners in a common ministry.

A legitimate question might be, "How does our congregation celebrate the ministries our members perform in the larger community?" A church council or governing board might spend some time asking how the congregation helps its members reflect on the spiritual and ethical dimensions of their professions and workplaces. The congregation could hold a special commissioning service for members who see their jobs and community volunteer service as a ministry of witness or reconciliation.

God's love is not limited to the church alone. It reaches out to the whole created order, which has ceased to acknowledge its Creator. If God's ultimate intentions include the healing of the whole cosmos, then we are agents of reconciliation in our neighborhoods and cities as well as inside our church walls.

Paul's emphasis on spiritual gifts draws us out of our narrow self-concern for institutional survival and triumphalist empire-building. It forces us to ask questions about how we manifest the Spirit's power in our everyday world. God does not give gifts so that the organized church may survive. God gives spiritual gifts so that a fallen world may experience grace and wholeness through the church's life of prayer and service.

EXERCISE TWO

Think for a few minutes about your own congregation. What are its most pressing needs?

Think about your community. What are its most pressing needs?

What specific gifts are needed to cope with these situations?

For each gift, list a person or persons (including yourself) whom you feel might have these gifts:

How could you or others "commission" these people so that their gifts could be better used for building up the church and the community?

≡≡≡

Chapter Three

How Can I Discover My Gifts?

P erhaps you now have some idea of the importance of spiritual gifts to the early church. You may also be grasping how crucial these gifts are for your own spiritual growth and development. These insights should prompt you to ask the next question: "How can I discover my own unique spiritual gifts for ministry?" Biblical figures such as Moses, Peter, and Lydia may provide us with some clues about discovering our own gifts.

Moses—Spiritual gifts are found through spiritual communion.

Moses' life illustrates how an ongoing life of prayer and meditation enables us to discern our gifts. Employment of spiritual gifts comes as a consequence of our communion with the One who bestows those gifts. Our doing *for* God arises from our being *with* God in prayer and meditation. We know our spiritual gifts and where to invest them when we first know and are known by the Giver of all life's gifts.

Moses' life illustrates the way we drift without purpose when we allow someone besides God to define our identity and life mission. Because he did not know the God who sustained his life, Moses knew neither who he truly was nor what he was created to do.

Moses had embraced the expectations of his adopted family. He was Pharaoh's son and an Egyptian prince. This identity, however, was congruent neither with his deepest self nor with God's purposes for him. He knew only the gods and goddesses of Egypt. He did not yet know the living God whose Word spoke him into being and called him for some specific service.

Moses eventually came to an awareness of his Hebrew origins. Pain and anguish accompanied this awakening. He murdered an Egyptian overseer and fled into the desert after his crime was discovered. He abandoned his old identity and way-of-being-in-the-world; but he had not yet met the God of Abraham and Sarah, of Isaac and Rebekah. He was still searching for a sense of identity and purpose.

Wandering in Sinai's wilderness, Moses met Jethro and his daughters. As he entered into their household, he found an identity that temporarily relieved his anxiety. Like his previous role as Pharaoh's son, this new self-definition pleased those around him, but it failed to satisfy Moses' own deepest yearnings.

He discovered his true identity and purpose only when he encountered God within the burning bush. Moses had to go *up* Mount Sinai and encounter the burning bush before he could *go out* into the world to accomplish God's purposes.

The same sequence occurred when Moses returned to Mount Sinai with the Israelites and received the covenant law. On the mountain, Moses encountered God and received the vision. He then came down the mountain and instructed the Israelites to build their sanctuary and their nation according to that vision.

Action flows from vision. Unless we have a vision of who we are and what gifts we possess, we cannot know what projects to undertake. Before we can go searching for places to use our gifts, we need to establish a loving communion between ourselves and the Giver of those gifts. Without this communication through prayer and meditation, the question "What are my gifts and where shall I use them?" is void and null. It is like saying, "I am getting married," without ever asking who it is you want to marry or why.

Sometimes men and women flee communion with God by trying to do things for God. They avoid communion with God by frantic efforts to do good and serve others. The recipients of their service inevitably find such people exhausting and alienating.

They actually have nothing to give. All we can ever give is ourselves. When our activity is an attempt to avoid confronting the God who speaks us into being, then our efforts bear no fruit and bring no satisfaction. "Fugitives need shelter. They cannot bestow it. And forgetting [their] own troubles in the service of others is in fact a euphemism for flight" (Williams, p. 23).

Bernard of Clairvaux must have had this in mind when he preached:

> If then you are wise, you will show yourself rather as a reservoir than as a canal. For a canal spreads abroad water as it receives it, but a reservoir waits until it is filled before overflowing, and thus communicates, without loss to itself, its superabundant water. . . . In the church at the present day, we have many canals, few reservoirs. (Steere, p. 85)

Successful mountain climbers say they must spend more time at their base camp in preparing for the climb than they spend in actually scaling the mountain. Their survival depends upon the base camp being well-provisioned and prepared. We cannot start scaling mountains of service unless our lives are firmly based in a life of prayer and communion with God.

In Eliot's play *Murder in the Cathedral,* Thomas à Becket worries that he is doing the right thing for the wrong reason. Is he standing up to King Henry because he wants to prove himself more important than the king and thus secure a place in history or because he wants to do God's will? The same question confronts us as we search for God's gifts and where to employ them. We must take care not to seek the right gifts for the wrong reasons.

We cannot truly know and employ our gifts unless we are rooted in a life of prayer and worship. Similarly, the way we use our gifts reveals the depth of our conversation with God. When our being with God does not help us identify our gifts for ministry and know where to put those gifts to work, then we must ask whether we are subtly resisting personal conversation with the living God. Faith in God without works for God is as dead as works for God without faith in God.

The Shakers had a saying: "Hearts to God, hands to work." "Hearts to God" means giving attention to the guiding vision we receive through prayer and Scripture meditation. "Hands to work" means putting our gifts to work so that the vision becomes a reality. We are doing the right things for the right reasons when both our hearts and our hands are moved by the same Spirit.

We are fond of quoting Irenaeus' statement that "the glory of God is a human being fully alive." We fail, however, to finish the sentence as Irenaeus wrote it: "The glory of God is a human being fully alive, and the full life of men and women is seeking God" (Ad. Haer. Book IV, 20:7). We cannot seek the joy of being fully alive—using all our gifts, talents, and senses as God intended—unless we are willing to dedicate our time, energy, and attention to seeking God in prayer, worship, and Scripture.

EXERCISE ONE ≡

In the space below, make an inventory of your spiritual disciplines. These disciplines are meant to foster communion with God, and from such communion comes a vision of our gifts and where to use them. Without this conversation and communication, efforts to identify our talents and gifts are little more than secular career-counseling techniques.

WHAT I AM DOING NOW	THINGS I MIGHT CHANGE
Participation in weekly worship	
Regular sharing in the Lord's Supper	
Daily prayer for self, others, and world	
Systematic reading of all the Scriptures	
Accountable discipleship through small-group support	
Fasting, tithing, and other classic disciplines	

Peter—God refocuses the abilities we already have.

The term *spiritual gifts* might mislead some people into thinking that spiritual gifts have nothing to do with natural abilities, whereas our natural abilities have to do with worldly affairs, our spiritual gifts take us beyond this world. Spiritual gifts are limited to extra-human phenomena such as speaking in tongues, visions, prophecy, or miracles.

As we saw in our study of Paul's letters, spiritual gifts certainly include extra-human signs and wonders. But Paul does not limit these gifts to such extraordinary occurrences. He goes on to list natural, mundane talents: giving, helping, serving, teaching, being hospitable.

Nowhere does Paul dichotomize gifts into spiritual and natural. He never limits spiritual gifts to something unworldly or useless for everyday survival. Rather, he implies that a spiritual gift is simply whatever comes from God and relates us to God. A spiritual gift for ministry is a personal strength which we recognize as a gift from God, given to strengthen the community and to reconcile a broken creation.

The difference between spiritual gifts and natural talents is not a difference in species. The distinction lies in "the viewpoint and intentionality of the possessor and user of the abilities. . . . If I think of my own abilities as natural talents and use them for self-gratification or for altruism, then they are simply human talents" (Edwards, p. 12). If, however, we see them as God-given abilities through which we share in God's continuing creation of community and cosmos, they are spiritual gifts.

Peter's story illustrates this point: Jesus identified some natural potential in Peter of which Peter himself was not yet aware. Jesus put Peter's existing skills to a new use. Peter remained a fisherman, but he no longer cast his nets in the Galilean Sea. From then on, he fished for human beings (Luke 5:1-11).

The same skills Peter used to manage his fishing business in Galilee would be employed for proclaiming the coming reign of God. "It is striking to see the shift that occurs in occupational activities from fishing to fishing for men [and women]. The call takes a person where he or she is and redirects his or her life. The talents and abilities already present are refocused and given meaning and have a place in the saving work of God for the people" (Lewis, p. 41).

God has created each of us with a unique configuration of abilities, experiences, and skills. We may choose to deny that these are God-given gifts and instead use them to promote our own status, wealth, and success. Or we may move beyond such self-centeredness and see our talents as divine gifts through which we have a share in God's saving work. In the first case, all we have are human, natural abilities. In the second case, we have spiritual gifts for ministry.

Lydia—Natural leadership gifts are converted to spiritual gifts.

Lydia represents another way God mobilizes the natural gifts we possess and refocuses them as spiritual gifts for ministry.

Lydia appeared in the story of Paul's missionary journey to Philippi. Paul and Silas entered Europe for the first time, bringing the gospel to a new continent. Lydia, from the city of Thyatira, was in the Philippian congregation. "The Lord opened her heart" and she responded to Paul's preaching.

Acts describes Lydia as a seller of purple goods (16:14). She was evidently a wealthy merchant, in charge of a large household of relatives, slaves, and friends. Her skills of organization, financial support, and leadership were now redirected. No longer used merely to make a living, they were employed for the upbuilding of the first European Christian community.

Lydia's home became the meeting place of the Philippian congregation. She was head of the house church that met in her home. She provided financial support for the church, oversaw its operation, and gave hospitality to Paul and other missionary travelers (Acts 16:40). Unexpected events and needs caused Lydia to put to God's service the skills and resources she previously had used for her own career and comfort.

Sometimes we are thrown into unexpected circumstances in which we encounter human needs that demand a response from us. Like Lydia, we find ourselves redirecting our talents, skills, and resources from worldly pursuits to those that further God's purposes.

Lydia, a successful merchant, had natural gifts for leadership and organization. She possessed financial skills that enhanced her household's wealth and prestige. After her conversion, she used these same natural abilities and talents as gifts for ministry. It was not so much that God gave her something she previously had lacked, but that her natural talents were redirected. They thus became spiritual gifts, gifts for ministry.

The same is true in our lives. We need to examine the natural talents and skills we possess. Then we must ask ourselves, "Am I using this ability for my own comfort and enjoyment or am I offering it to God's service?"

EXERCISE TWO

The following exercise will help you begin to classify your natural talents and inclinations. Once you begin to gain some clarity about them, you must decide how you will commit yourself and your skills to God, who can transform them from human talents into spiritual gifts for ministry.

Imagine you are in a large room. Six groups have formed in various places. Each group contains people with similar interests. You want to be with people who like the same things you like, so you must pick one of these groups (exercise inspired by Holland, 1985). Which group will you join?

1.
People who have athletic or mechanical ability and like to work with tools, machines, objects.

4.
People who like to learn, analyze, solve problems.

2.
People who have clerical or numerical ability and like to work with data. They like to follow through on others' instructions.

5.
People who have artistic, innovative ability and like to work in unstructured situations.

3.
People who like to work with people to influence, persuade, or manage, so that institutional goals are accomplished.

6.
People who like to work with people to inform, train, cure, teach. Usually they like working with words.

Which group would you most enjoy joining? With which group would you feel most uncomfortable? How would you rank the remaining groups between your first and last choices?

This exercise helps you to broadly identify where you could best use your gifts. It is unlikely that someone with artistic gifts who likes to work in unstructured situations would find spiritual fulfillment as a church treasurer or trustee. Similarly, someone who likes to work with machines and tools is not a good candidate for teaching seventh-graders.

In light of the above exercise, what are some places in your church or community which you feel might become places of ministry for you? Does this exercise help you understand why you felt unhappy while doing a certain task or holding a certain office in your congregation? You might have thought the problem was the church or even that you were the problem. In fact, the issue was a mismatch between your gifts and the task.

EXERCISE THREE

The word *enthusiasm* comes from two Greek words—*en Theos,* or "in God." Our enthusiasms can reveal those places where God is at work in us. In the areas in which we are uniquely gifted, we are *en Theos.* Our enthusiasms can help us better pinpoint our gifts.

The following exercise asks us to identify experiences we found fulfilling or enjoyed.

In the space below, list fifteen to twenty events in your life which you enjoyed and found fulfilling. These may be from your work career, your leisure-time or volunteer activities, or school experiences.

Do not try to evaluate or critique your list as you write it. Simply list as many events as you can without judging or prioritizing them. Then take a few minutes to reflect on the list and see if you can add any others.

Go back through your list and circle the five to ten events or experiences you found most fulfilling. Note those experiences below in the left-hand column. In the right-hand column, write the talent, quality, or skill you needed in that particular situation.

Be specific. If you say your talent is "helping," then include how or who or what you helped. Is it helping people? Helping organizations achieve goals? Helping by organizing data or information? The categories in the first exercise may help you be more specific.

Go back over your list of talents and qualities. Are there patterns or constellations of abilities? Are there relationships between skills or talents? Again, be as specific as you can. Write your observations in the space below.

You now have a list of your personal strengths. Like Peter's, these qualities are potential gifts for ministry. They are more than natural abilities. If you have not done so already, think about what needs to happen in order for you to recognize them as God's spiritual gifts, meant for building up the community and the cosmos. How can you invest those gifts in God's continuing creation?

Our wounds may become our gifts.

Every gift has its shadow. The shadow of the gift of love is possessiveness. Virtue can become twisted into self-righteousness. The gift of administration degenerates into control and oppression. Paradoxically, our greatest strengths are often our greatest weaknesses. When we misuse the most precious and special gift which God has bestowed upon us, we experience that gift as a temptation and weakness. What was meant to relate us to God and to give us a share in God's continuing co-creation becomes something we use for our self-aggrandizement.

Another way to discover our gifts is to examine what we see as our greatest weaknesses. Sometimes we experience the shadow side of our gifts before we identify the positive qualities. Our faults come more readily to mind than our gifts. Yet those failings and flaws provide clues to our gifts. Hidden behind our sins and temptations are untold riches. That which we experience as a wound or weakness is only a fallen, distorted image of the spiritual gift with which God has most blessed us.

We sometimes ask God to take away or to destroy those things that we experience as our temptations. We are perplexed when God does not answer our prayers. We begin to wonder if God really cares about us when our weaknesses persist. Yet if our most unique spiritual gifts for ministry are the mirror images of our weaknesses, God cannot take away what tempts us without also depriving us of what was created as special and unique in us.

Rather than ask God to remove our temptation, we should ask God to heal our *misuse* of the gift to which the temptation points. "By asking God to kill the central block and problem, we have been asking God to kill our most divine and unique inner gift, the most living and creative part of our selves" (Wuellner, p. 50).

Jesus had the ability to see the gifts hidden behind the sinful weaknesses of men and women. He saw the gift of compassion and love obscured by Mary Magdalene's sexual life. He saw the gift of leadership behind Peter's impulsiveness. He saw, behind Paul's zeal for the Law, a gift for evangelism and spreading the gospel. Jesus knew that a sinful weakness was only the shadow side of God's most precious gift. Through forgiveness and grace, Jesus healed the wounded misuse of the gift so that his followers could offer in God's service that which was most uniquely theirs.

The same truth applies to our lives. Our possessiveness and jealousy can be healed, revealing the gifts of love and compassion. Our inertia, and indifference, when healed, release gifts of peace, faith, and integrity. Our perfectionism and compulsive control of others can be transformed into the gift of leadership and apostleship. Our anger masks our gift of prophetic passion for justice and righteousness.

When we are trying to identify our spiritual gifts, we need to look at more than our successes and strengths. We must explore the temptations that have wounded us. Those weaknesses and temptations, in fact, may reveal clues to our most profound and beautiful gifts.

Exploring our wounds, however, is not easy. It is difficult to look at our failings and faults. It is even more difficult to examine the wounds we have experienced through suffering and pain.

A spiritual guide once asked me to keep track for one month of all the things that brought tears to my eyes. Some tears may be tears of joy or tenderness. Others may flow because of sorrow or pain. Still others come to our eyes over quite unremarkable circumstances, without any warning. Nonetheless, they all reveal what has stirred us at the very depths of our being. They disclose where God is at work in the roots of our lives. Our tears, our sufferings, and our wounds provide clues about God's purposes and gifts.

We instinctively believe that we should work from our strengths and hand on to others the riches we possess. Instead, we sometimes offer our most precious gifts when we operate from our weaknesses. With empty hands we pass on what we do not possess, producing effects we cannot explain. Through our sufferings and wounds, we heal others. Thus Paul writes in Second Corinthians 4:8, 10-12:

> We are afflicted . . . but not crushed . . . always carrying in the body the death of Jesus, so that the life of Jesus may also be manifested in our bodies. For while we live we are always being given up to death for Jesus' sake, so that the life of Jesus may be manifested in our mortal flesh. So death is at work in us, but life in you.

In our wounded suffering and inadequacy, we mediate something to others that is not our own possession but a gift passing through us to others. Through our wounding experiences, "we discover new and hitherto unknown and unimagined areas of our being. We discover that the self we took as our total self was in fact only a small fraction of what we are" (Williams, p. 153).

Much of our human uniqueness is related to the specific wounds and pains we have experienced. Our suffering and failures have shaped and molded us. They have made us aware of things to which we otherwise would have remained blind. They have toughened and strengthened us as we discovered resources for enduring and coping which otherwise would have remained untapped. Moreover, no two people share the same wounds and sufferings. Each of us has our own unique pattern of wound-prints.

Thus our wounds and sufferings may reveal our gifts. When we honestly face those experiences that have wounded us, we may discover within them a certain graceful gifted-ness. Because whatever is given becomes a gift. Even our sufferings have hidden gifts within them.

The unique configuration of our wounds and what we have made of those wound-prints reveals God's spiritual gifts for our lives. "Our gifts are gained at a price, a price that we have already paid in our life's wounds and suffering. If we had not suffered the particular and unique set of wounds we have, we would not have the particular and unique set of gifts we now possess" (Edwards, p. 91).

EXERCISE FOUR

List below those behaviors, emotions, passions, or weaknesses you experience as your greatest tempta-tions. Try not to pass judgment on yourself or on them; simply write them down without evaluating or criticiz-ing.

Now go back and circle the two or three temptations you would rank as most powerful in your life and list them in the left-hand column below. In the right-hand column, turn that weakness on its head. What strength, positive quality, or value does it become?

TEMPTATION	VALUE OR QUALITY WHEN REVERSED

Spend some time in prayer about your weaknesses and temptations. Ask God to reveal whether your temptations are simply distortions of your gifts. What would need to happen in your life for those gifts to be healed and restored to God's original intentions? Write your resolutions and reflections in the space below.

Chapter Four

Where Shall I Employ My Spiritual Gifts?

B y now, we should have some perspective on our actual and potential spiritual gifts. Our exercises on family messages and childhood heroes or heroines have helped us clarify the way our unique family experiences shaped a certain configuration of gifts within us. The exercises on accomplishments and enthusiasms have helped us obtain another perspective on our talents. Perhaps the reflection on wounds and suffering has brought to light some gifts that otherwise would have remained unacknowledged and unused. Our work with biblical gifts has provided still another lens through which to look at our lives.

Before we move on, we need to summarize and consolidate what we have learned about our gifts so far. Use the chart below to draw your various insights together.

GIFTS I AM SURE ABOUT	GIFTS I THINK I MAY HAVE

From my family experiences

From my accomplishments and enthusiasms

From my wounds and temptations

From encounter with New Testament gifts

As you look at your summary, you may realize how far you have come in identifying your spiritual gifts. But only half the task has been accomplished. The most important part is yet to come. Until we discover where God wants us to employ them, our spiritual gifts remain barren and sterile.

Gifts are given so we may share in God's co-creative work. If we have received gifts but are not using them, then we have abused what God so generously bestows. When our abilities and talents are at work where the world needs them, we are using God's gifts as they were intended. Frederick Buechner states it clearly in *Wishful Thinking:*

> The kind of work God usually calls you to is the kind of work (a) that you need most to do and (b) that the world most needs to have done. If you really get a kick out of your work you've presumably met requirement (a), but if your work is writing TV deodorant commercials, the chances are you've missed requirement (b). On the other hand, if your work is being a doctor in a leper colony, you've probably met requirement (b), but if most of the time you're bored and depressed by it, the chances are you have not only bypassed (a) but probably aren't helping your patients much either.
>
> (p. 95)

We've spent considerable time identifying our gifts. Now we need to look just as carefully at where God wants us to employ our gifts in our broken world.

Parable of the Talents: Use it or lose it.

Jesus tells a parable in which he highlights the issue of using our God-given talents where they yield the greatest dividend of healing and wholeness. Matthew (25:14-30) and Luke (16:1-13) give different versions of this parable, but both make the same point.

When a man was going on a journey, he called his servants together and gave them some of his property. One servant received five talents; another, two; still another, one talent. The servant who received five talents traded them wisely and made another five. The second servant used his two talents resourcefully and doubled his investment. The third servant, however, buried his single talent in the ground.

Eventually, the master returned and asked for an accounting. He was pleased with the first servant: "Well done, good and faithful servant; you have been faithful over a little, I will set you over much; enter into the joy of your master." Reviewing the second servant's dividends, the master complimented his behavior and repeated his promise.

To the third servant, however, the master said, "You wicked and slothful servant! . . . So take the talent from him, and give it to him who has the ten talents. For to every one who has will more be given, and he will have abundance; but from him who has not, even what he has will be taken away."

The parable's ending seems unfair. The one-talent servant loses what little he possesses. When we think about it, however, that is exactly what happens in our lives. When we fail to use our natural abilities, we lose them. If we stop jogging or exercising for a few weeks, our muscle tone deteriorates rapidly. When we don't use it, we lose it.

The same principle applies to our spiritual gifts. Each one of us receives some talent or gift from God. God has given this divine property into our hands. The master's property is not always evenly distributed, but everyone gets something. Our gifts will vary: Some of us receive more talents than others; some talents are more prominent; some have more worldly value. But whatever we have, we are expected to invest wisely.

When we fail to use our gifts, we are depriving ourselves of the opportunity to be all we were meant to be, and we are also depriving God of an expected return on the divine investment. This may be what Mark 3:29 means when it speaks of blasphemy "against the Holy Spirit." We engage in blasphemy when we do not use the gifts God has bestowed upon us through the Spirit.

The parable's expectation is clear: Use your talents and abilities in God's service. God has given us talents and gifts so that we can multiply God's good works in the world. We encounter God's judgment when we fail to invest our gifts in the world to accomplish God's healing purposes:

> "Very truly, I tell you, the one who believes in me will also do the works that I do and, in fact, will do greater works than these, because I am going to the Father. . . . And I will ask the Father, and he will give you another Advocate, to be with you forever." (John 14:12, 16 NRSV)

It is not enough to know our gifts. We must also invest them so they will produce a dividend of *shalom* in our wounded and violent world. Our gifts call us out of the fearful self-centeredness in which our talents are seen as means to make money, to buy security, to acquire status and prestige. Instead, our God-given gifts for ministry invite us into faithful discipleship, following Christ in our daily work and vocation.

EXERCISE ONE ═══════════════════════

This is an exercise used by the Laity Project at Andover-Newton Theological Seminary. It is a helpful way to think about your particular "world" and the various processes, structures, and organizations into which it is segmented.

In Ring 1, write the persons, groups, or situations that are priorities in each segment of your world. Some sections may have more items than the others. If you cannot think of any names or situations for a particular section, just leave it blank for now.

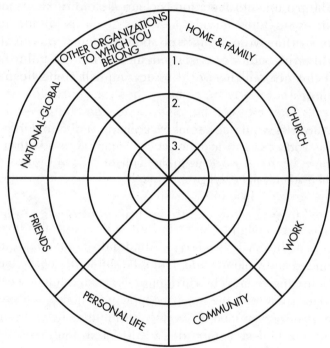

Additional Notes

You should come back later, however, and reflect on what that blank space means: What are you avoiding in that part of your life? What are you missing out on? Is there some pain or some fear at work here?

In Ring 2, write your wishes for each person or situation. What would you like to see in this section of your world that is different from the way it now exists? If you could project into the future an ideal state or condition, what would it be?

In Ring 3, write the gifts or special talents you possess that might help make your wish a reality. Again, the object is not to fill every open segment with some word or phrase. There may be some wishes for which you have no gifts. You may, on the other hand, feel that several of your talents would be useful in realizing a different ideal.

Instead of trying to fill in every segment, ask what the pattern of responses suggests about where your gifts coincide with the world's needs.

Parable of the Talents: Be faithful in little gifts first.

Jesus' parable of the talents highlights a second point about our spiritual gifts and the world's needs. The master tells the first two servants, "You have been faithful over a little, I will set you over much" (Matt. 25:21). Luke contains the same statement with a slightly different wording: "Whoever is faithful in a very little is faithful also in much; and whoever is dishonest in a very little is dishonest also in much" (Luke 16:10 NRSV).

If you are not faithful in doing the small things, how can God entrust the really important ones to you? If you don't use the information you already have, then why should you expect to receive any more insight or illumination? Before we can embark on our special, unique mission in life, we must be faithful in the basics of Christian discipleship.

We share some parts of our Christian calling with all other Christians. Until we are faithfully living out that vocation, we cannot expect God to entrust us with something uniquely our own.

> If you aren't trying to bring more gratitude, kindness, forgiveness, honesty, and love into the world each day, you can hardly expect that you will be entrusted with the Mission to help bring peace into the world or anything else large and important. If we do not live out our day by day Mission in the valley, we cannot expect we are yet ready for a larger mountaintop Mission. (Bolles, p. 305)

Some parts of God's vision for our world are too big to be entrusted to any one Christian. Paul makes a clear distinction between spiritual *fruit* and spiritual *gifts*.

The fruit of the Spirit is a ninefold cluster of graces which relate to the moral virtues. These have to do with our relationships and our quality of being. Spiritual gifts, on the other hand, have to do with our functions in ministry.

All Christians share in a common calling to bear spiritual fruit. Such fruitfulness does not require any special spiritual gifts. So it is not appropriate to avoid our responsibilities for bearing the fruits of love, joy, peace, patience, self-control, or goodness by saying, "I don't have a gift for that."

And unless we are faithful in bearing spiritual fruit, we cannot be entrusted with spiritual gifts. Our doing must flow from our being. John Wesley had a practical rule for judging extraordinary spiritual gifts. No claim to an extraordinary gift should be rejected out of hand; nonetheless, all such gifts should be judged by the person's spiritual fruits: love, joy, peace, patience, kindness.

Spiritual gifts without spiritual fruit become destructive. They become self-serving personal possessions rather than instruments through which we serve God by serving God's world. Bearing spiritual fruit keeps us God-centered, so that our spiritual gifts are not distorted into a means of self-aggrandizement. Without the spiritual fruit of love, kindness, or gentleness, spiritual gifts can become tools to manipulate others, to exercise power over them, to control their spiritual and moral development.

Unless we are faithfully discharging our common Christian calling of bearing spiritual fruit, we cannot expect to receive our unique calling to exercise our spiritual gifts.

EXERCISE TWO ═══════════════════

Paul provides a list of spiritual fruits in Galatians 5:22. He counterpoints each fruit with a corresponding sin. Since Christian life is always a process of becoming, rather than of static accomplishment, most of us fall somewhere in the middle of these two extremes.

Spend some time experiencing the tension between these two poles as you work with the chart below. Mark where, on the continuum of 10 to 1, you would place yourself. Why?

Love	10	5	1	Indifference
Joy	10	5	1	Bitterness
Peace	10	5	1	Anger
Patience	10	5	1	Impatience
Kindness	10	5	1	Envy
Goodness	10	5	1	Impurity

Faithfulness	10	5	1	Disloyalty
Gentleness	10	5	1	Cruelty
Self-control	10	5	1	Greed

Ask yourself the following questions:

1. Which fruit is most evident in my daily life?

2. Which fruit is least apparent?

3. Which fruit is the easiest to practice?

4. Which fruit is the most difficult to practice?

5. Where would you like to be in your bearing of spiritual fruit after six months? What do you need to do to be there?

We can share Jesus' hidden life.

Mark's Gospel contains a theme known as the Messianic Secret. As Jesus healed and cast out demons, he commanded the people not to reveal his identity. They were not to disclose who healed them: "And [Jesus] sternly charged him, and sent him away at once, and said to him, 'See that you say nothing to any one; but go, show yourself to the priest, and offer for your cleansing what Moses commanded, for a proof to the people' " (Mark 1:43). Just as Jesus' identity and divine purposes remained hidden to others' eyes, so the effects of our ministries sometimes remain hidden to others. Sometimes they remain hidden to our own eyes.

In the Sermon on the Mount, Jesus reminded his disciples to fast, pray, and give alms in secret. They were not to parade their good deeds on the street corner. Instead, they were to go into a secret closet to pray; and their God, who dwells in a secret place, would hear them (Matt. 6:1-18).

We might spend our lives bearing spiritual fruit and exercising our spiritual gifts. Yet no one would realize the impact of our gifts upon the world. We ourselves may never see the consequences of our work and witness. Yet we should never doubt that we have touched some lives and done God's work. When a stone is cast into a pond, it sets up ripples that radiate outward in all directions, touching shores the stone never imagined.

So it is with our lives. We are like small pebbles cast into the sea of life. Our lives create patterns of energy and experience which wash upon shores we never dreamed possible. We do not know the ripple effect of our lives upon other people and events. Only when we meet God face-to-face will we know the difference our gifts have made both in God's own life and in the lives of men and women around us.

Loren Eiseley speaks of the "spectral wars" we fight throughout our lives. When a friend asked Eiseley what he did while he was university provost, Eiseley took him to a corner of the campus where the road had a curious shape.

"That," said Eiseley to his friend, "was a move in the spectral war." When he first came to the university, the corner of 34th Street and Walnut allowed trucks to cut a short left turn. Because it was a busy corner, students and bicyclists frequently were hit by trucks. As provost, Eiseley made it a point to attend the planning committee that was discussing campus street improvements. His testimony was convincing, and now an extended corner is at that spot. Trucks cannot make a short left turn there.

"And this is all you remember of the provostship?" asked his friend.

"It's really quite enough," replied Eiseley. "You see . . . that old short corner here at Walnut gave death a better edge, a percentage. I like to think, though I don't know them, that every year there are people left alive because of what I did about the corner. That's what I call the spectral war. It's unseen, but it's everywhere" (Eiseley, 204-5).

Whenever we use our spiritual gifts, we are placing our lives at the service of the One who gives life to the world. We are fighting the forces that deal death. We may never know the consequences of our work, but our efforts silently help to tip the balance in favor of life over death.

I copied some words into the front of my Bible long ago. Unfortunately I have lost the exact reference. They may have come from the sermons of John Henry Cardinal Newman or they may be from some anonymous source. Regardless of who said them, they are worth pondering:

God has created me to do some definite service.
God has committed some work to me, which God has
not committed to another.

I have my mission. I may never know what it is in this life. But I shall be told in the next.

I am a link in a chain, a bond of connection between persons. God has not created me for nothing. I shall do good. I shall do God's work.

Each of us shares in a common Christian vocation of bearing spiritual fruit, witnessing to God's love, kindness, peace, and joy in a violent, alienated world. Each of us also has some special calling, for which God has implanted certain spiritual gifts into our genetic inheritance, our unique configuration of abilities, and our life experiences. We may never know in this life what purpose or difference those fruits and gifts make in the world. But we shall know it when we meet God face-to-face.

Study Guides
for Group Leader

Session One

1. Have participants introduce themselves and share one or two significant facts about themselves. Suggest that each participant answer a question such as, What unique talent, interest, or skill do you think you might have?

2. Begin with a time of prayer and worship. An appropriate hymn would be "Lord God, Your Love Has Called Us Here" (*The United Methodist Hymnal*, #579). The worship leader might stress that God has called each of us to some ministry or service which no one else can fulfill. We are not called by some merit in us, but by God's grace and love. During the next few weeks, we will be working together to glimpse God's call to ministry in our lives (see vs. 3 of the hymn). After a time of open prayer, the leader might close with the following from the *Book of Worship* (p. 241, emended): "O almighty God, who in your mercy has redeemed the world by the love of Christ: Call many men and women to the ministry of your church, so that by their labors your light may shine in the darkness, and the Reign of Christ may be hastened through the perfecting of your people; through Jesus Christ our Lord. Amen."

3. On a sheet of newsprint, suggest some group norms. These norms specify the rules of behavior for the group. They should include:

- Confidentiality. Whatever is said within the group meeting remains in the room and is not repeated elsewhere.

- The meetings will begin and end on time. Participants are expected to be present at the starting time.

- If participants will be absent, they should contact the group leader so that the group can begin without them.

- The group will share equally in discussion time. One or two members should not monopolize the discussion, leaving little time for others.

- There will be an attitude of openness and acceptance. We are present to help one another grow, not to criticize or correct others' opinions.

4. Distribute the books and explain that participants should read the chapters and do the exercises between meetings.

5. Set the schedule of meetings.

6. Dismiss with a prayer.

Session Two

1. Review the group norms.

2. Begin with a time of worship, reading in unison Psalm 139:1-18. Ask participants to meditate silently upon a word, phrase, or verse of the psalm that speaks to them. After a time of silence, invite them to speak aloud their word, phrase, or verse. At the close, read the psalm again in unison.

3. Divide into small groups and ask participants to share their time lines. Ask the groups to discuss these questions: What does your life and experience suggest to you about a spiritual gift for ministry that is uniquely yours? What can you offer to others out of your unique personal experience?

4. One of the chapter's themes concerns Jeremiah, Isaiah, and other prophets who tried to flee their gifts, but whom God persistently put into situations where they were forced to use that gift. Have participants discuss times when they have found themselves in situations they believed were too much for them—when they were expected to do something they never thought they could do—yet found surprising resources and strengths within themselves. Ask them what this might suggest about the gifts God is inviting them to offer as ministry.

5. Ask participants whether it was easy or difficult to identify family sayings. Were they surprised by the things they remembered? How is their present life shaped by the messages they received as children? Are these still appropriate or should they move on, putting away childish things?

6. Ask participants to share a significant hero or heroine. What do these suggest about each participant's spiritual gifts?

7. Close with a prayer or hymn, possibly "Here I Am, Lord" (*The United Methodist Hymnal*, #593).

Session Three

1. Open with worship, using First Corinthians 12:4–13:13 as an appropriate scripture. A visual symbol should represent the way, as Christians, we are part of one Body. Participants could join hands as the scripture is read. Or a ball of yarn could be passed among participants, each taking hold of the string and passing the ball on, until the whole group is linked by the single strand of yarn. Or embody in some other way Paul's idea of being one Body, bound together in love. Sing "We Are One in the Spirit, We Are One in the Lord."

2. Review the exercise that asks participants to identify a biblical gift. What was difficult about this exercise? What was easy? What did you learn?

3. Ask participants if they feel that their community service, homemaking, or jobs are places of ministry for them? Or is ministry something that goes on only inside the church? Why or why not? What could the church do to better support those who see community service, home, or work as their ministry?

4. How does your congregation's committee on nominations and personnel work? Do you feel you are just asked to fill slots? Does the committee convey that it is only the institution's needs that matter? Do you feel the committee seriously tries to help members identify their gifts and find ways they can grow spiritually through their service? What could be done differently?

5. Close with a time of prayer for one another.

Session Four

1. An appropriate Scripture for worship and meditation might be Isaiah 53. Stress how we find healing through Christ's wounds. Christ is a wounded healer, and God calls us to offer our woundedness as a source of healing ministry for others. During a time of prayer, ask participants to voice their prayers of petition, intercession, and thanksgiving for times of temptation, hurt, woundedness, and healing.

2. Divide participants into small groups to share their exercises on spiritual disciplines. What are they doing now and what might they change? Ask participants to write on a 3 x 5 card one change they would like to make. Be sure they do *not* write their names on the cards. Collect the cards, shuffle them, and redistribute them, making sure everyone gets someone else's card. Invite each participant to pray daily for the person whose card they hold. They should pray that the person will receive the grace to implement the desired change.

3. Invite participants to share what they learned about their spiritual gifts from the exercise on experiences they have enjoyed. Was this easy to do or difficult? Why? What did it help them discern about their spiritual gifts that they did not know before?

4. Do participants agree with the idea that our temptations are the flip side of our strengths? How is this a helpful way to think about temptations and personal faults? How is it not helpful?

5. What did participants learn about their spiritual gifts from the exercise on temptations?

6. What did participants learn about their spiritual gifts from the exercise on wounding life experiences? Invite them to share stories about ways they have been helped through a personal crisis or tragedy by someone who has been through it and survived. How can we play that role for others?

7. Close with "Lord, You Give the Great Commission" (*United Methodist Hymnal*, #584).

Session Five

1. You may want to open this last session with a brief prayer, and then close with worship and Holy Communion.

2. Read the quote by Buechner on page 74 and ask participants if they agree or disagree. Why or why not?

3. Discuss the distinction between spiritual gifts and spiritual fruit. Is this an important distinction? Why or why not? Can you have one without the other? Why or why not?

4. In small groups, ask participants to share their responses to the exercise on spiritual fruit. What did they learn about themselves? What would they like to change? Do they have a plan or strategy for change?

5. Ask participants to share in small groups the results of their chart from the beginning of chapter four. What gifts do they believe they have? Which ones do they think they might have? Which of these come from family experiences? From accomplishments and enthusiasms? From wounds and temptations? From Paul's lists of spiritual gifts? Now that they know their gifts, where will they employ them? Ask them to write, on a sheet of paper, a plan for using their gifts, put the sheet of paper in an envelope, and address it to themselves. Explain that you will collect the envelopes and mail them after six weeks. The letter will serve as a covenant and reminder about their plans. (Do this only if you plan to follow through and actually mail the letters!)

6. Ask the group what it means that someone has been praying about their situation during the week. What has it meant for them to be praying for someone else?

7. Close with Holy Communion. An appropriate closing litany or prayer might be "The Prayer of Saint Francis" (*United Methodist Hymnal*, #481).

Bibliography

Bolles, Richard N. *What Color Is Your Parachute?* New York: Harper & Row, 1988.

Buechner, Frederick. *Wishful Thinking*. New York: Harper & Row, 1973.

Capps, Donald. *Deadly Sins and Saving Virtues*. Philadelphia: Fortress Press, 1987.

DeTourville, Abbe. *Letters of Direction*. Oxford: A. R. Mowbray & Co., 1984.

Dunning, James B. *Ministries: Sharing God's Gifts*. Winona, Minn.: St. Mary's Press, 1980.

Edwards, Lloyd. *Discerning Your Spiritual Gifts*. Cambridge: Cowley Press, 1988.

Eiseley, Loren. *All the Strange Hours*. New York: Charles Scribner's Sons, 1975.

Holland, John L. *Making Vocational Choices*. Englewood Cliffs, N.J.: Prentice-Hall, 1985.

Küng, Hans. *The Church*. New York: Image Books, 1976.

Lewis, Roy. *Choosing Your Career, Finding Your Vocation*. New York: Paulist Press, 1989.

O'Connor, Elizabeth. *Eighth Day of Creation: Gifts and Creativity*. Waco, Tex.: Word Books, 1971.

Steere, Douglas. *Prayer and Worship*. Richmond: Friends United Press, 1978.

Steindl-Rast, David. 1983. *A Listening Heart*. New York: Crossroad Press.

————. 1984. *Gratefulness, the Heart of Prayer*. New York: Paulist Press.

Traherne, Thomas. *Centuries, Poems, and Thanksgivings*, ed. E. M. Margoliouth. Oxford: Clarendon Press, 1958.

Whitehead, James D., and Whitehead, Evelyn E. *The Emerging Laity*. New York: Image Books, 1988.

Williams, H. A. *True Resurrection*. New York: Harper & Row, 1972.

Wuellner, Flora S. *Prayer, Stress, and Our Inner Wounds*. Nashville: Upper Room Books, 1985.